D0587616

Danish Flower Thread

The Danish Handcraft Guild's fine embroidery thread is known throughout the world for its smooth texture and soft, subtle shades. The 100 colours available all coordinate and blend to create attractive, naturalistic effects.

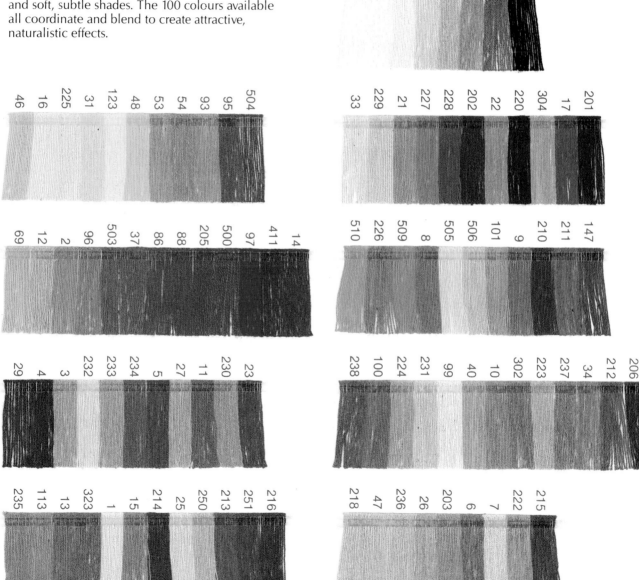

Cross Stitch
for
Christmas

Anne Marie Petersen

MEREHURST
LONDON

Contents

Published 1990 by Merehurst Limited
Ferry House, 51/57 Lacy Road, Putney, London, SW15 1PR
By arrangement with Forlaget ULO, Copenhagen
Printed in Denmark by Clausen Offset, Odense.

© Forlaget ULO, Copenhagen, and
  The Danish Handcraft Guild, Copenhagen.

Text: *Anne Marie Petersen*
Photographs: *Mikael Müller*

ISBN 1-85391-173-9

It's Christmas again ...

The Christmas season itself lasts officially for twelve days. But in Denmark, as in many other countries, it seems to begin earlier every year. Today, the month of November has hardly begun before our attention is drawn to the approach of the Yuletide festivities. Magazines contain articles with recipes for Christmas cakes and other sweets and instructions for making Christmas decorations and embroideries. Shops send out catalogues with ideas for Christmas presents, and the streets are decorated with evergreens and coloured lights.

The Danes are especially fond of Christmas; If it didn't exist, they would have to invent it - if only to brighten the long, dark winter. In these northern latitudes the days during December are extremely short, and the winter weather can be very depressing, lacking the crisp snow and bright sunshine enjoyed in neighbouring Nordic countries.

To take their mind off the surrounding gloom, the Danes retreat to the cozy warmth of their homes. They close the curtains, light a fire in the fireplace, and invite some friends or relatives to come round for coffee and pastry or a glass of toddy. Besides enjoying good conversation, they may work on a beautiful piece of embroidery, which can then provide additional pleasure as a Christmas decoration.

Ideas for presents

A handmade Christmas present is a pleasure to give and to receive. The thoughtfulness and the hours of work that go into the present make it especially cherished by the recipient; and for the giver, the work itself can be very satisfying, especially if it is done while chatting with friends.

Embroidered items make lovely presents. On these pages are some possibilities, including jam jar covers embroidered with berry motifs, a spectacle case with a delicate bird-on-a-branch design and a cosy for forcing a hyacinth bulb. Bookmarks are simple projects, which could be used to introduce a child to the pleasure of embroidery.

Covers for jam jars, *embroidered with strawberries, blackcurrants, blackberries, raspberries, rowan berries and cherries*

4

Tissue case

Cosy for a hyacinth glass

Pincushion

Bookmarks

Clutch bag

Spectacle case

5

The Advent wreath

Many people think that the weeks leading up to Christmas are the best part of the holiday season. Among the pleasures of this time is that of putting up the Christmas decorations. In Denmark, on the first Sunday in Advent, the Advent wreath is lit.

It is hung in the most attractive corner of the sitting room or over the dining room table, where it can be seen and admired by everyone during the Advent season. Made of natural materials from the forest, it can be a real work of art, especially if hung with beautifully embroidered ribbons.

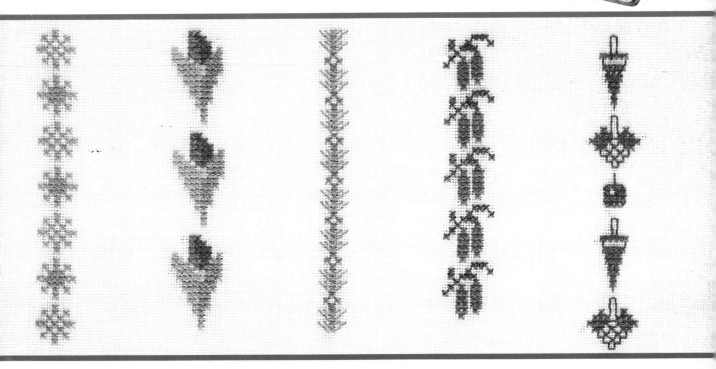

Ribbons for the wreath. *Embroidered ribbons are used to hang up the Advent wreath. The same motifs can be used to make pretty bookmarks.*

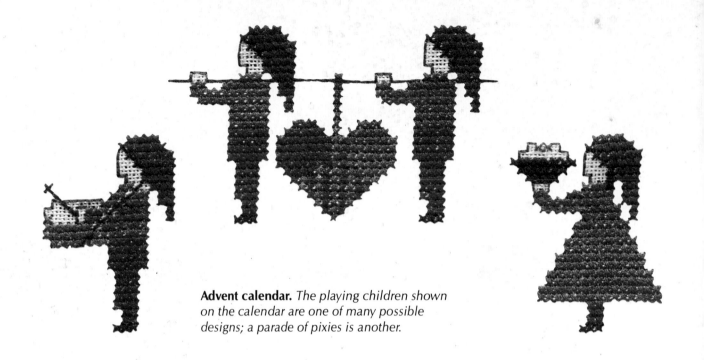

Advent calendar. *The playing children shown on the calendar are one of many possible designs; a parade of pixies is another.*

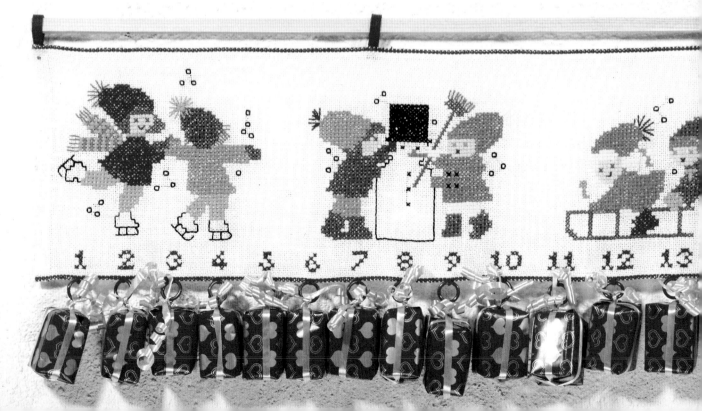

The Advent calendar

The Advent calendar is a favourite European Christmas tradition. Children enjoy opening the little windows to count the number of days remaining before Christmas.

In Denmark, a variation of the Advent calendar - the present calendar - has recently become popular. Below each date is hung a little present in colourful wrappings, one for each day from the first of December to the 24th. The presents are neither large nor expensive, but small things of a more practical nature, such as pencils, glue, tape or the occasional sweet. The pleasure

comes from expectation and the unwrapping, rather than from the value of the present itself. Some families choose to give a special toy on Sundays which the child then can unwrap and play with, so that the parents can sleep on undisturbed.

Many Danish homes have also introduced the tradition of the Christmas stocking, from Britain and North America. This is similar to the Advent calendar custom. Each morning in the month of December one small present is placed in the stocking which the child then unwraps.

The Christmas stocking *has become very popular with children in Denmark. The design at the top could be used around a stocking or simply as a picture.*

Christmas cards

The custom of sending Christmas greetings by post is as popular in Denmark as in English-speaking countries. Large numbers of Christmas cards are sent to relatives and friends at home and abroad. Some people make their own cards. These may contain photographs of the children, showing how much they have grown since the previous year. For a very special card, which will be kept and treasured, one can work a small motif in cross stitch and insert it in a paper frame. Cards may be displayed in a long row on a table or sideboard, forming an attractive Christmas decoration. A new custom is to keep the cards in an embroidered bag, especially useful if space is limited. Two examples of these Christmas bags are shown here.

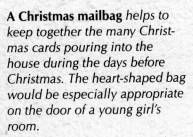

A Christmas mailbag *helps to keep together the many Christmas cards pouring into the house during the days before Christmas. The heart-shaped bag would be especially appropriate on the door of a young girl's room.*

Christmas cards. *The small motifs are relatively quick to work and make very welcome presents.*

The Christmas table

In ancient pagan times, when the Danes worshipped the old Nordic gods Odin and Thor, the winter solstice, the 22nd of December, was a time of great rejoicing. Later, after Christianity was introduced, the lengthening of the days provided another cause for celebration in the joyous Christmas season.

In Denmark, as in other countries, good food is an important part of the festivities, and a beautifully laid table enhances the sense of occasion.

The best china, crystal and cutlery are brought out, as well as treasured pieces of needlework: the Christmas tablecloth, napkins, table runners and placemats. Some are decorated with traditional Danish motifs, such as pixies, evergreen branches, angels and candles — others, with more stylized and abstract patterns.

It is a special pleasure to bring out the rarely used heirlooms worked years ago by a mother or grandmother, perhaps including the first piece of embroidery she made for her new home. But it is also satisfying to create something new for the Christmas table and to make your own contribution to the family's collection of beautiful needlework.

15

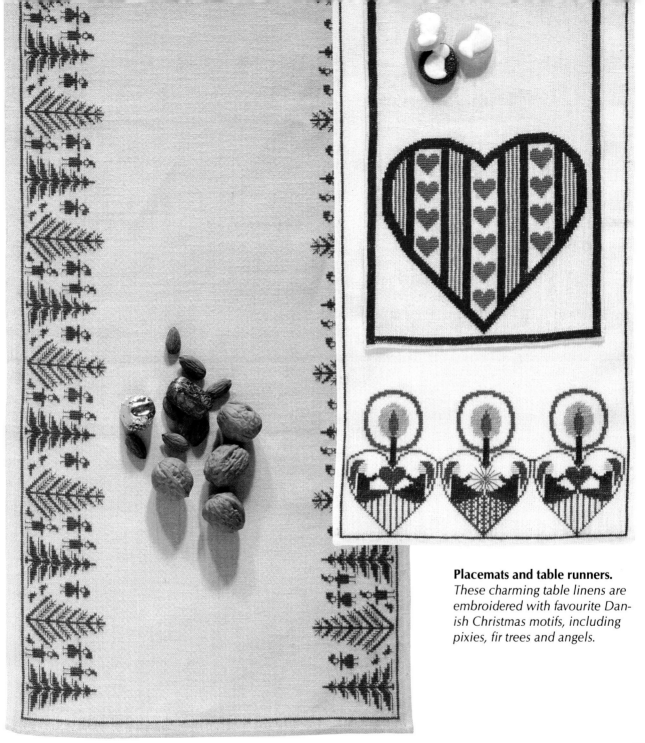

Placemats and table runners.
These charming table linens are embroidered with favourite Danish Christmas motifs, including pixies, fir trees and angels.

17

Table mats and Christmas pictures. *Table mats in a variety of shapes and sizes are extremely useful as well as decorative. Here are several, embroidered with a graceful holly garland, jolly little elves and a stylized Christmas wreath; on the next page, some more modern designs. Even matchboxes can be given a festive air with cross-stitched motifs.*
The embroidered pictures depict the journey of the three Wise Men, following the star, and the Nativity scene itself.

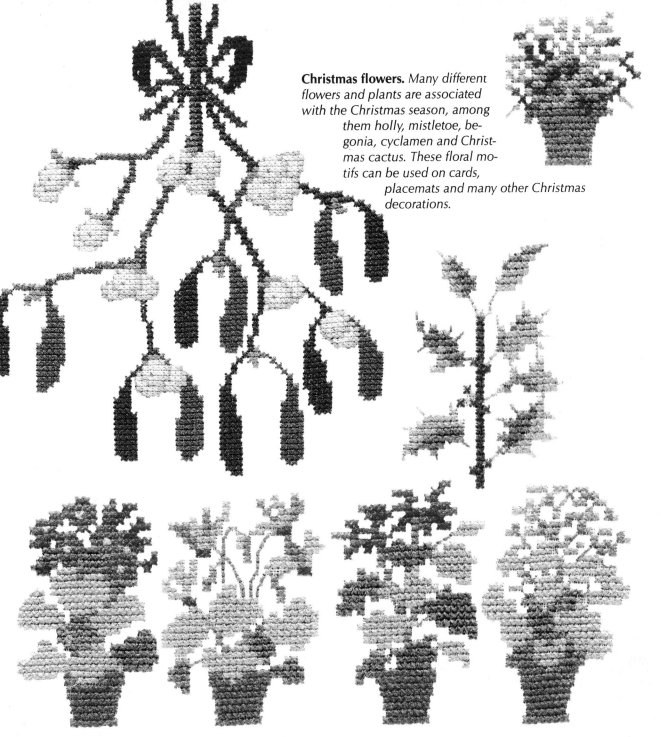

Christmas flowers. *Many different flowers and plants are associated with the Christmas season, among them holly, mistletoe, begonia, cyclamen and Christmas cactus. These floral motifs can be used on cards, placemats and many other Christmas decorations.*

The Christmas tree

The tradition of the Christmas tree goes back, in Denmark, to the middle of the last century. The tree is lit on the 24th of December, and people dance around it with joined hands and sing the old Christmas carols. In Denmark it is still the custom in many homes to use real candles on the tree, even though this demands extra care and preparation, in the form of filled buckets of water. Many families still select their own tree in the forest, fell it and take it home, where it is decorated according to their own favourite tradition. Some people make their own tree ornaments, such as the embroidered cornets and heart shapes shown on this tree.

Embroidered Christmas ornaments *in heart-shaped mounts.*

If there are children in the family, some Christmas cookies on the tree are essential.

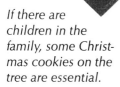

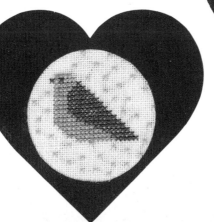

23

Cornets *are made from a pattern which is actually a quarter of a circle. By joining four identical cornet patterns one gets a round table mat matching the Christmas tree decorations.*

The Christmas tree cloth

An important accessory in homes where real candles are used on the tree is
the Christmas tree cloth. This protects the floor or the carpet from wax stains,
and makes vacuuming the shed needles much easier. Because it must be
hard-wearing, the Christmas tree cloth is made of hessian (burlap)
or some other kind of strong fabric.

In Denmark it is the custom to dance around the Christmas Tree.
This illustration shows a typical Danish Christmas scene from the mid-nineteenth century.

Danish Cross Stitch Embroidery

Many countries have a tradition of cross stitch embroidery. It figures prominently in the peasant costume of many Central European countries, for example. In Britain and the United States it was used extensively in the samplers produced in the 19th century, and it remains popular in those countries today.

Nowhere, however, is cross stitch more popular than it is in Denmark. Danish cross stitch designs range from bright, cheerful stylized motifs to subtly detailed naturalistic embroideries.

The Christmas designs given in this book are typically fresh and appealing. They were created by artists of the Danish Handcraft Guild, an organi-zation founded in 1928 in order to promote and encourage artistic Danish needlework, hand-crafts and domestic arts. The Guild is under the patronage of Her Majesty Queen Ingrid.

All of the cross stitch embroidery projects in this book are available in kit form from the Danish Handcraft Guild's agent in England: Danish Embroidery Club, Mikiko Yamanashi, 63 Walton Street, London SW3 2HT, England.

The designs have been created for specific projects, such as placemats, tree ornaments and Christmas cards. However, many of them could be adapted to suit other items; and, of course, you could in many cases use colours different from the ones shown.

Cross stitch can be worked on all fabrics with countable threads. The stitches should cover the background fabric completely, so it is important that the weight of the embroidery thread be suitable for the fabric chosen. If the thread is too heavy, the result will be clumsy, and if it is too thin, the coverage will not be adequate. The stitches must be even and smooth. It is easy to check the stitch tension by holding the work up to the light. If lines of light are visible between the rows of stitches, the tension is too tight. If the tension is too loose, the stitches will stand out from the surface. A cross stitch, which is normally worked over two fabric threads both horizontally and vertically, consists of two superimposed diagonal stitches. Cross stitch can be worked in

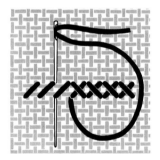

Cross stitch in horizontal rows. *Work from left to right, completing all under-stitches first. Each under-stitch passes diagonally over 2 threads, from the bottom left to the top right corner. The over-stitch is worked on the way back. Each over-stitch passes diagonally over 2 threads, from the bottom right to the top left corner. On the reverse side of the embroidery, only vertical stitches can be seen.*

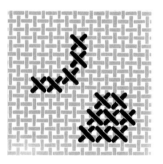

Cross stitch in vertical lines or staggered. *Work down-wards from top. Each stitch is completed before the next one is begun. Work all under-stitches in one direc-tion, and all over-stitches in the other. Only vertical stitches appear on reverse side. A cross stitch can be staggered 1 thread in re-lation to stitches already sewn. Rows of stitches can be staggered 1 thread in re-lation to each other, too.*

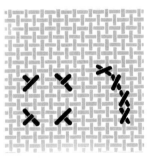

Asymmetrical and partial cross stitches. *Depending on the design, cross stitches can be sewn asymmetrically by, for example, shortening one »arm« of the stitch or »compressing« the stitches in one direction or the other.*

On the left are shown four ¾ cross stitches, and on the right, half or long cross stit-ches passing over 2 threads in one direction and only 1 in the other direction.

horizontal and vertical rows. For horizontal rows, stitch the desired number of under-stitches from left to right first. Then work the over-stitches on the return. After the last over-stitch, bring the needle up two threads below the finished row, ready for the next row. For vertical rows, complete each stitch individually and bring the needle up two threads farther down for the next stitch.

There are two important rules for cross stitch work. First, the under- and over-stitches respectively must always slant in the same direction. The stitches are worked towards oneself. If the design demands it, the work may be turned around completely (180°), but it must never be turned a quarter turn (90°), because the stitches will then slant in the wrong direction. Second, with both vertical and horizontal cross stitches one must never skip over more than the space of two stitches (= 4 threads) in the same row or the long loose threads lying on the reverse side may show through. Staggered or asymmetrical cross stitches are used to create more naturalistic outlines. A half cross stitch, the under-stitch only, can also be used for this purpose.

Backstitch worked in an unbroken line is particularly well suited for outlines. The needle comes through the fabric one stitch from the beginning of the line to be worked. It goes back to the beginning of the line and comes through again one stitch beyond the starting point. Single back stitches are used for fine details.

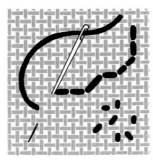

Backstitches *are worked in unbroken lines. The stitches can be sewn in straight lines or diagonally over 1 or 2 threads.*
Single backstitches are sewn over 1 thread intersection or over a single thread.

Stem stitch is another linear stitch which is extremely suitable for sewing rounded lines, for example, stems of flowers. Sewn close to each other, stem stitches can also be used to fill large areas of fabric.

Fabric. Cross stitch is worked on evenweave fabric — that is, fabric having the same number of threads per inch, or centimetre, in both directions. Evenweave may be made of linen or cotton, and it comes in a variety of weights, ranging from 14 to 36 threads to the inch. For the projects in this book, three different weights of fabric are specified: 18, 26 and 30.
Another type of evenweave, called Aida cloth, is woven from groups of threads, about 11 to the inch. On this fabric each stitch is worked over one intersection of threads. Hessian (burlap) is an unbleached linen evenweave with about 10 threads to the inch.

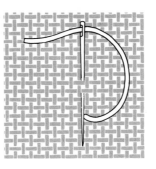

Stem stitches *slanting to the right are worked upwards. Bring the needle through, place the thread on the right side of it, insert the needle into the fabric 1 stitch length up and bring through one half stitch down.*

Needles. Use a blunt-ended tapestry needle for the work: No. 24 for the two finer fabrics and no. 22 for the coarser. A crewel needle or a sharp needle is used for the finishing.

Thread. Different kinds of thread may be used for cross stitch embroidery. It is important to match the thickness of the thread to the weight of the fabric, so the stitches are clearly defined while still covering most of the fabric.
The recommended thread for Danish cross stitch designs, including those in this book, is Danish Flower Thread, a fine, matt-finish, single-strand cotton. If you are unable to obtain Danish Flower Thread, we suggest that you substitute a stranded cotton floss by matching the shades of Danish Flower Thread specified with the projects to the colour chart in the beginning of this book.
For working on hessian

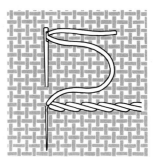

Corner stem stitch. *Insert the needle into the fabric in the corner with the last whole-length stitch, and finish with a half-length stitch. Bring the needle through; start again with a half-length stitch as shown.*

burlap), a fine crewel, single-stranded wool yarn is recommended.

Washing and ironing instructions. The recommended threads are dyed with long lasting colours. However, the thread may contain some surplus dyeing colour which will run out when the embroidery is washed. Therefore, it is important to observe the following instructions.
Wash the embroidery by hand or machine in tepid water on the delicate cycle. Use a mild detergent without bleaching agents. Place the work between two white sheets and lay flat to dry. Do not dampen and roll up the embroidery before ironing. Instead, place it wrong-side up on the board, over a soft cloth, dampen a thin cloth, wring it out thoroughly, place it on top of the embroidery, and iron until the top cloth is dry. Then iron directly on the back of the embroidery.

29

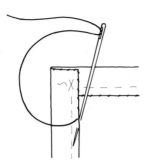

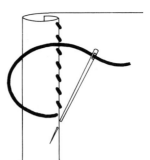

Hem with right-angled corners (*suitable for cotton and fine linen*).
*Mark out the depth and width according to finished measurements. Count 7 and then 6 fabric threads for the two turnings on all four sides of the embroidery. Make a crease with your fin-*ger or with a needle along the threads where the linen is to be folded. Cut off the corners as shown, and fold the fabric once, keeping the hems in place with pins. Fold the second hem and tack (baste) it into place. Sew the hem with invisible stitches.*

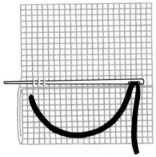

If you prefer, you may work hem stitch on the hems; here hem stitch is shown worked over 3 threads.

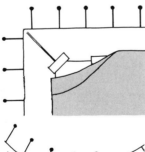

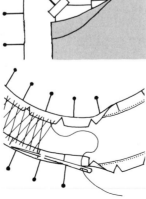

On smaller items, instead of using glue, lace the hems together as shown.

Slip stitches. *Draw a thread to mark the two fold lines of the hem; fold and tack (baste) along these lines. Insert the needle between the two layers of fabric and up through the folded edge. Draw the thread through, not too tightly. Work a couple of stitches on top of each other to fasten on. Work downwards from the top. Insert the needle diagonally from the right through the bottom layer of fabric, 3-5mm (¼ - ⅛") down from the last stitch, while at the same time passing it under 3-4 threads and out through the folded edge. Pull the stitch taut. Take the needle into the fabric another 3-5mm (¼ - ⅛") farther down and continue in this way.*

Mounting on cardboard.
Mark out the height and width according to the specified finished measurement, and cut out a corresponding piece of cardboard. Pin the embroidery onto the cardboard with right side outwards, and fold the fabric tightly around the cardboard. Glue the corners in place, then fold and glue one side at a time and let it dry. Finally, glue a piece of paper onto the back.

Instructions for the designs

Page refers to the page of the book on which the finished object is shown. The numbers following the page number refer to the different patterns and should be used if you want to order embroidery kits from the Danish Handcraft Guild.
Fabric. The recommended type of evenweave fabric is specified by weight — given as the number of threads per inch.
Size. The finished size is given in centimetres and inches. You will need to add about 5cm (2") to all edges when cutting the fabric to allow for seams and hems. When following the instructions use either centimetre measurements or inches, but do not mix the two.
Thread number. The number given opposite a symbol refers to a shade of Danish Flower Thread.
The columns show which stitches are used in the designs. Unless otherwise stated, a single column indicates that only cross stitch is to be used. Two columns represent backstitch (left) and cross stitch; 3 columns represent backstitch (left), half cross stitch (middle) and cross stitch (right).
Technique. Unless otherwise instructed, use 1 strand of Danish Flower Thread. One square on the grid equals 4 thread intersections on the fabric — that is, one cross stitch. Find the middle of the pattern by means of the arrows. Start working from here.
Finishing. The instructions are given with each design.

FABRIC: *26 white*   **SIZE:** *Diameter 18cm (7")*   **DESIGNER:** *Gerda Bengtsson*

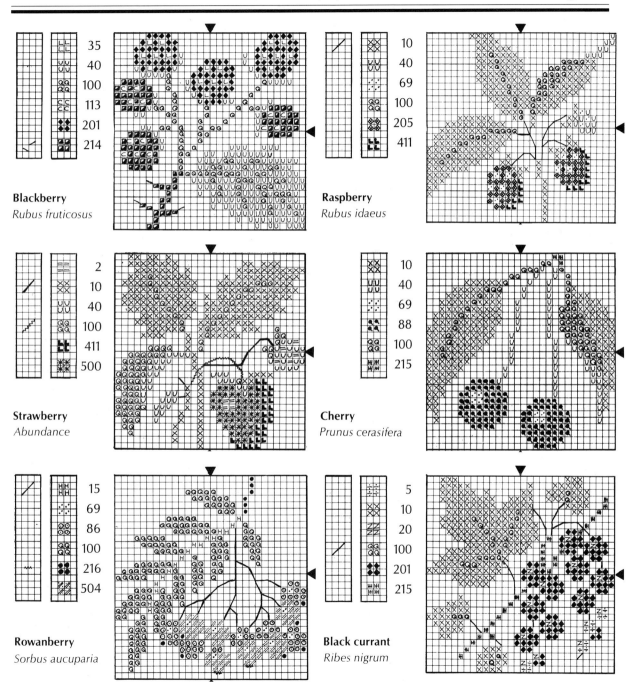

Blackberry
Rubus fruticosus

L L / L L	35
U U / U U	40
Q Q / Q Q	100
C C / C C	113
◆ ◆	201
2 2 / 2 2	214

Raspberry
Rubus idaeus

✕ ✕ / ✕ ✕	10
U U / U U	40
∴ ∴	69
Q Q / Q Q	100
✪ ✪ / ✪ ✪	205
L L / L L	411

Strawberry
Abundance

= = / = =	2
✕ ✕ / ✕ ✕	10
U U / U U	40
Q Q / Q Q	100
t t	411
✶ ✶	500

Cherry
Prunus cerasifera

✕ ✕ / ✕ ✕	10
U U / U U	40
∴ ∴	69
⬤ ⬤ / ⬤ ⬤	88
Q Q / Q Q	100
H H / H H	215

Rowanberry
Sorbus aucuparia

H H / H H	15
∴ ∴	69
◎ ◎	86
Q Q / Q Q	100
⬤⬤ / ⬤⬤	216
⁄⁄ / ⁄⁄	504

Black currant
Ribes nigrum

∴∴ / ∴∴	5
✕ ✕	10
Z Z	20
Q Q / Q Q	100
◆ ◆	201
H H / H H	215

1 = 37 (101) (205)   **4** = 227 (202) (88)

2 = 53 (228) (37)   Outline and bottom edge = **4**

3 = 223 (510) (11)   Inner edges = **3, 1, 2**

TECHNIQUE

Work in stem stitches. At upper right-hand corner of fabric measure 3cm (1¼") in and down. This point corresponds to the arrow on the pattern at left; begin here. Use 2 strands of Danish Flower Thread or 4 strands of floss.

FINISHING

Press the embroidery from the reverse side. Cut 2 pieces of iron-on interfacing, each 22 x 43cm (8¾ x 17"), and iron one piece at a time onto the reverse side of the embroidery. Trim the linen to 2cm (¾") from embroidery. Fold and turn under the linen close to the embroidery, and sew it to the side with herringbone stitches. Cut out and iron a piece of white cotton for lining 27 x 48cm (10½ x 18¾"). Fold under and press 2.5cm (1") at all edges. Tack (baste) the lining right side out to the reverse side of the embroidery. Overcast with small stitches all the way around, 2 threads from the edge. Fold the bag along the line forming the bottom (A). Overcast sides together one thread from each side, using 2 strands of the colour used for the edge.

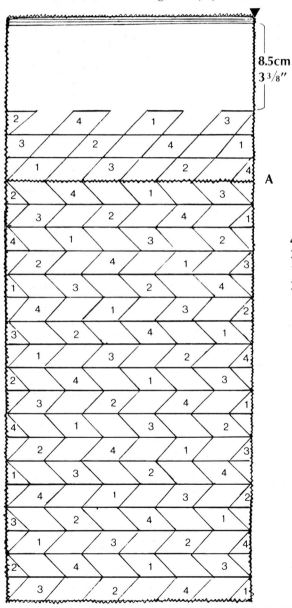

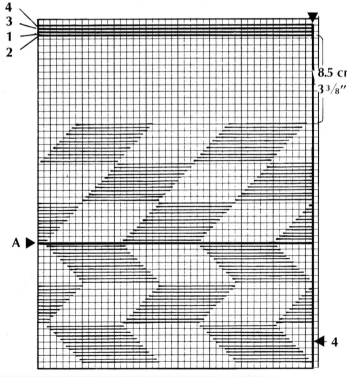

FABRIC: *30 white*   **SIZE:** *10 × 17cm (4 × 6¾")*   **DESIGNER:** *Christiane Hæk*

TECHNIQUE

Cut 2 pieces of linen, each 20 x 25cm (8 x 10").
Find the middle of the shorter side of the linen. Measure 4cm (1½") down from the edge, and start the embroidery at the arrow on the pattern.

FINISHING

Iron 2 layers of fusible interfacing onto each of the 2 pieces of linen. Cut the sides to fit.
Fold under the sides 4 threads from the embroidery; fold the top and bottom only 2 threads from the embroidery.
Join sides and bottom from the right side using slip stitch.
If you want to use a lining for the case, it must be sewn onto the 2 pieces of linen before the sides are joined.
Sew a narrow decorative cord along the edge of the case.

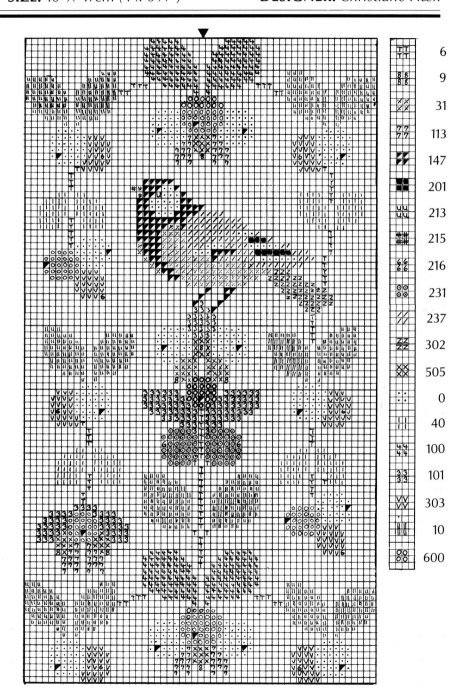

TT / TT	6
88 / 88	9
XX / XX	31
77 / 77	113
▨▨	147
■■	201
UU / UU	213
## / ##	215
66 / 66	216
00 / 00	231
// / //	237
ZZ / ZZ	302
XX / XX	505
·· / ··	0
III	40
44 / 44	100
33 / 33	101
VV / VV	303
IIII	10
00 / 00	600

PAGE: *5*
FABRIC: *26 white*   **SIZE:** *4 × 24cm (1½ × 9½")*   **DESIGNER:** *Gerda Bengtsson*

TECHNIQUE

Find the middle of the shorter side of the linen. Measure 3cm (1¼") down from the edge. Start the embroidery at the arrow on the pattern.

FINISHING

Leave 3cm (1¼") at each end for fringes. Machine stitch around the work. Fringe the ends. Trim sides close to stitching; overcast. Fringe ends.

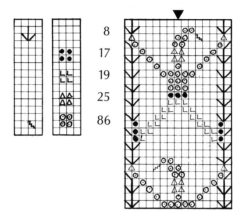

8
17
19
25
86

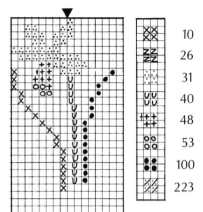

10
26
31
40
48
53
100
223

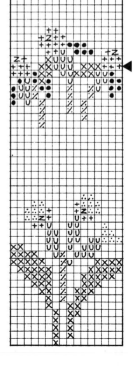

PAGE: *5*   **DESIGNER:** *Else Hansen*
FABRIC: *Aida*   **SIZE:** *9 × 12cm (3½ × 4¾")*

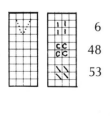

6
48
53

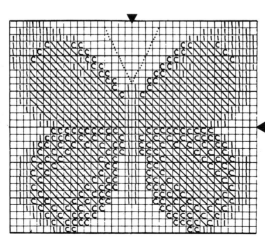

34

FINISHING

Iron fusible interfacing onto the reverse side of the embroidery. Cut away the fabric 2cm (¾") from the embroidery on the short sides and 1cm (⅜") on the long sides. Fold and turn under the fabric 5 threads from the embroidery. Fold the seams on the short sides twice, making them 1cm (⅜") wide. Fold the case so that the edges meet in the centre, and join the sides by overcasting them with fine stitches.

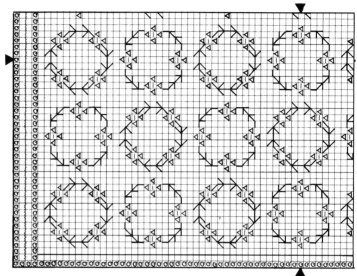

= =	48
▲▲	510
⊖⊖	100

TECHNIQUE

Cut a piece of fabric, 25 x 30cm (10 x 12"). Make a full-size tracing paper pattern, following the outline given. Place the centre of the shape on the centre of the fabric. Tack (baste) the outline to the fabric, including the centre line. Tear away the paper gently. Start the embroidery at arrow on pattern and at centre of the fabric.

FINISHING

Press the embroidery on the reverse side, remove the centre line thread and iron interfacing onto the reverse side. Trim fabric to 1cm (⅜") from outline at the sides and close to the embroidery at the bottom. Sew bias binding at bottom, sew the cone together on reverse side and turn right side out.

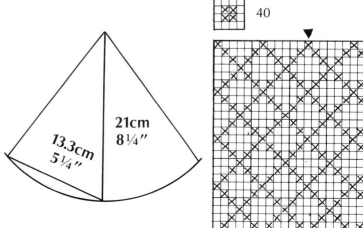

✕✕	40

13.3cm 5¼"   **21cm 8¼"**

35

TECHNIQUE

Cut 4 pieces of linen, each 5 × 75cm (2 × 29½"). Find the middle of the short side of the linen. Measure 3cm (1¼") down from edge. Start the embroidery at the arrow on the pattern.

FINISHING

Fold under 5mm (¼") of fabric at each side, 5mm (¼") from the embroidery, and sew in place. Fold the side seams to the reverse side with an additional turn, so that they meet in the middle. Sew on a button loop, 3.5cm (1½") long, at each end of the band.

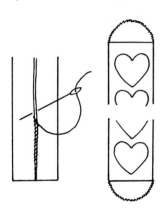

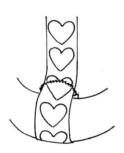

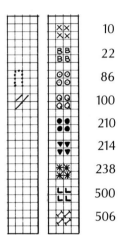

	X X / X X	10
	B B / B B	22
	O O / O O	86
	Q Q / Q Q	100
	● ● / ● ●	210
	▼ ▼ / ▼ ▼	214
	✳ ✳ / ✳ ✳	238
	L L / L L	500
	✕✕ / ✕✕	506

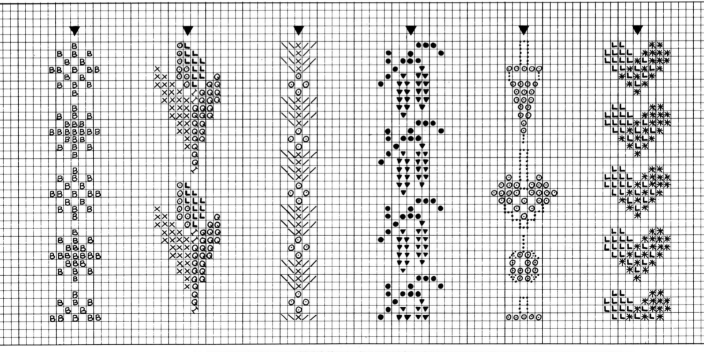

FABRIC: *30 white*   **SIZE:** *4 × 21cm (1½ × 8¼")*   **DESIGNER:** *Ida Winckler*

TECHNIQUE

Find the middle of the short side of the fabric. Measure 3cm (1¼") down from edge. Start the embroidery at the arrow on the pattern.

FINISHING

Fold a double hem along each side, with the second fold 1 thread from the embroidery so that they meet. Join them with overcasting.

Reserve 3cm (1¼") at each end for fringes. Machine stitch across the ends at these points, then remove the threads for the fringed edges.

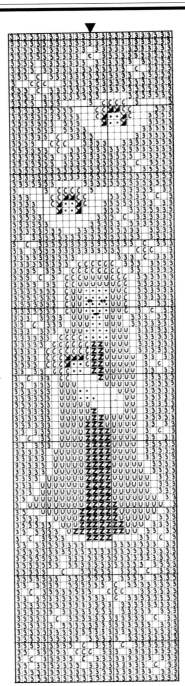

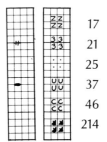

Z Z Z Z		17
3 3 3 3		21
· · · ·		25
U U U U		37
C C C C		46
◤◥ ◣◢		214

TECHNIQUE

Work with 2 strands of Danish Flower
Thread or 4 strands of floss.
Work a single row of cross stitch in
red, about 3cm (1¼") up from the
lower edge, for a distance of 94cm
(37"). Find the middle of the long side
of the fabric. Count 4 threads up from
the red line. This point corresponds to
the arrow on the pattern. Begin the
embroidery here. Work another line of
cross stitch about 2.5cm (1") above the
embroidery.

FINISHING

Fold under and hem the fabric 1.5cm
(⅝") from the embroidery. Turn under
the top and bottom edges outside the
borders. Work 5 button loops for
hanging up the calender. Sew a small
ring under each date; the packages
can then be fastened to these rings.

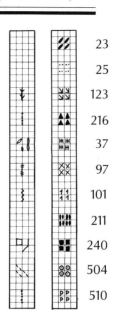

		23
		25
		123
		216
		37
		97
		101
		211
		240
		504
		510

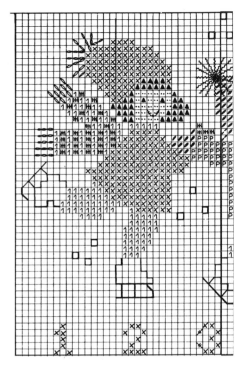

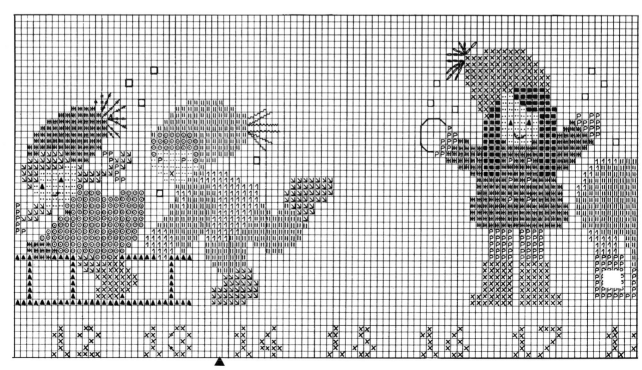

39

PAGE: *10*
FABRIC: *18 white*
SIZE: *16 × 96cm*
   (6¼ × 38″)
DESIGNER: *Ingrid Plum*

TECHNIQUE

Work with 2 strands of Danish Flower Thread or 4 strands of floss.
Work a row of cross stitch in red, 3cm (1¼″) up from lower edge, for 96cm (38″). Count 4 threads up from red line. This point corresponds to the arrow. Begin the embroidery here. Work another row of cross stitch 2.5cm (1″) above the embroidery.

FINISHING

Fold under and hem the fabric 1.5cm (⅝″) from the embroidery at sides. Turn under top and bottom edges outside borders. Work 5 button loops for hanging. Sew a small ring under each date for packages.

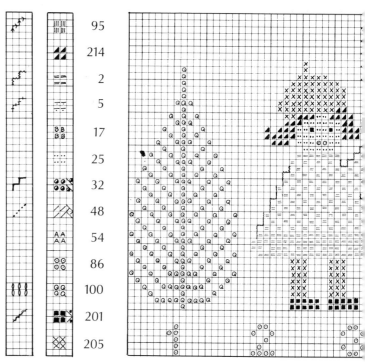

		95
		214
		2
		5
		17
		25
		32
		48
		54
		86
		100
		201
		205

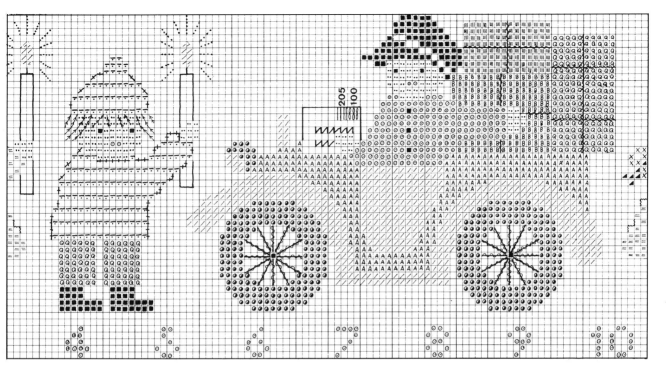

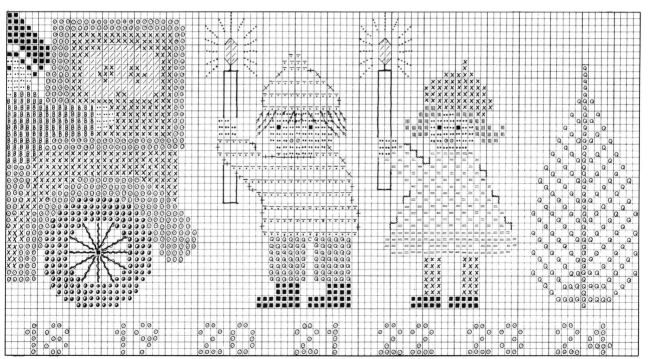

41

FABRIC: *26 white*   **SIZE:** *8 × 24cm (3 × 9½")*

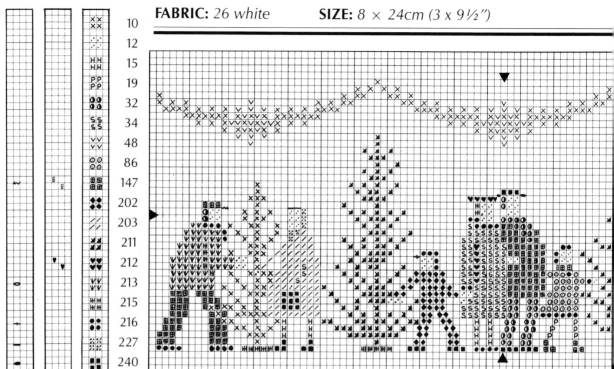

PAGE: *11*

FABRIC: *18 white*   **SIZE:** *8 × 24cm (3 × 9½")*   **DESIGNER:** *Edith Hansen*

TECHNIQUE

Work with 2 strands of Danish Flower Thread or 4 strands of floss.

FINISHING

Turn under and press edges. Slipstitch to top of stocking.

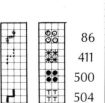

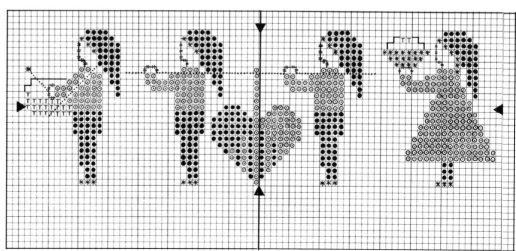

TECHNIQUE

You will need at least 30cm (12") of fabric. Work with 4 strands of Danish Flower Thread or 8 strands of floss.

FINISHING

Iron fusible interlacing onto the fabric. Make a heart pattern of the dimensions shown; fold paper first for symmetry. Use it to cut a heart from the fabric. Cut out the heart. Cut out the pocket 1cm (³⁄₈") from the fabric, size 18 × 18cm (7 × 7"). Sew bias binding onto the two upper sides of the pocket. Place the pocket on top of the heart, and sew bias binding along all sides of the heart. Place a 20cm (8") long loop of folded bias binding at top of the heart, between the heart and top of pocket.

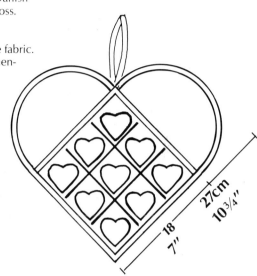

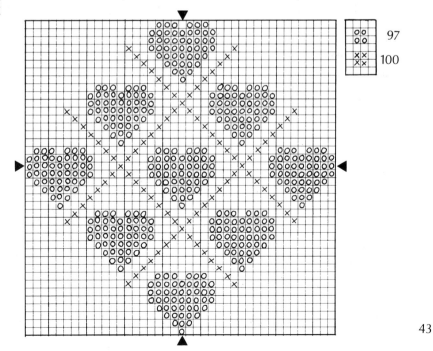

oo / oo	97
xx / xx	100

43

FABRIC: *18 white* **SIZE:** *22 × 24cm (8½ × 9½")* **DESIGNER:** *Ida Winckler*

TECHNIQUE

Work with 2 strands of Danish Flower Thread or 4 strands of floss.
Find the middle of the short side of the fabric. Measure 5cm (2") down from edge. Start at arrow.

FINISHING

Cut a piece of fabric the same size as the embroidered piece. Place pieces right sides together, and machine stitch around the bottom and side edge, 3 threads from the embroidery. Fold a double top hem 8 threads from the embroidery, 3 threads wide, and sew it in place. Sew button loops or rings onto the corners to hang up.

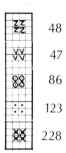

ZZ ZZ	48
VV VV	47
88 88	86
∴∴	123
XX XX	228

PAGE: *13*
FABRIC: *26 white*
DESIGNER: *Ida Winckler*

FINISHING

Cut the fabric a little larger than the window of the card and glue it onto the card for forming the back, positioning design correctly in relation to the window. Glue the front card in place.

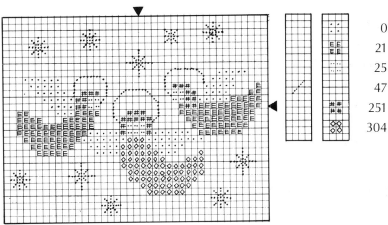

	0
	21
	25
	47
	251
	304

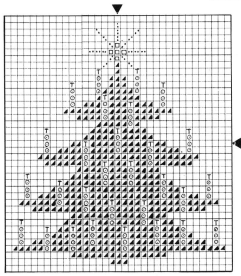

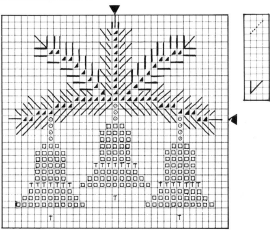

	47
	53
	86
	100

		2
		10
		40
		100
		210
		240
		411
		500

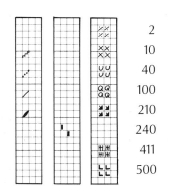

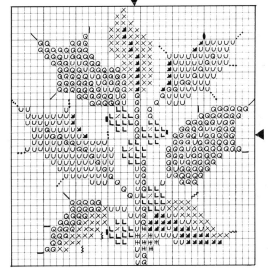

45

TECHNIQUE
Work with 2 strands of Danish Flower
Thread or 4 strands of floss.

FINISHING
Turn up a 2.5cm (1″) hem using hemstitching, worked over 3 threads.

●● ●●	86
✕✕	503

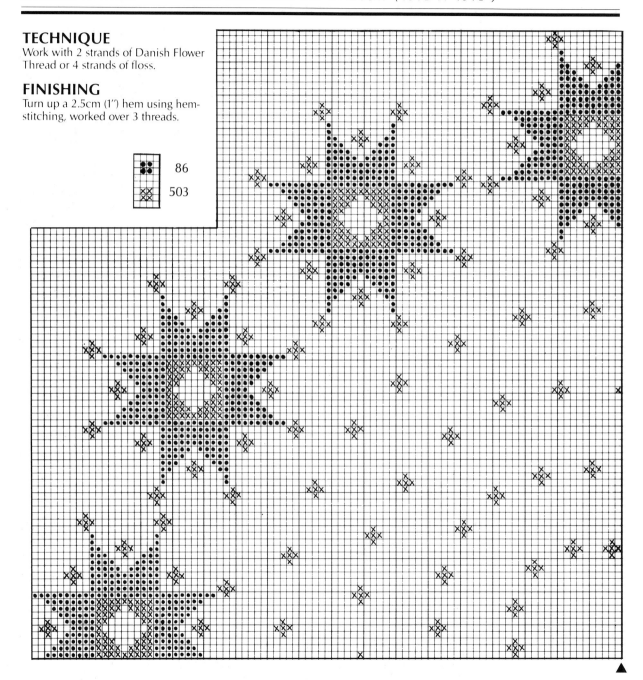

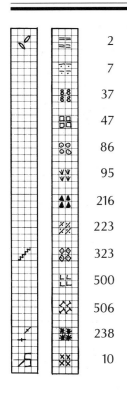

	2
	7
	37
	47
	86
	95
	216
	223
	323
	500
	506
	238
	10

PAGE: *17*
FABRIC: *26 white*
SIZE: *Runner 33 × 98cm*
(13 x 38½")
DESIGNER: *Ida Winckler*

TECHNIQUE

Measure 5cm (2") up from the short side. Start at the arrow.

FINISHING

Trim fabric to 21 threads from embroidery. Fold and turn under a double hem, 7 threads wide, 7 threads from the embroidery, and sew it in place with small hemming stitches.

  86

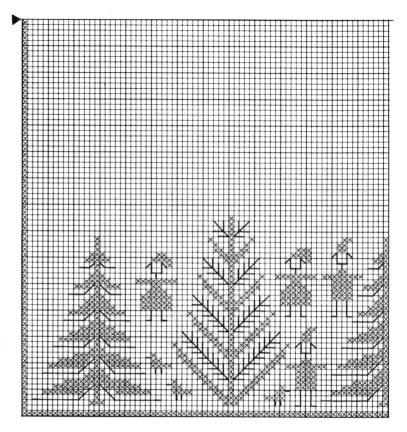

PAGE: *16*

FABRIC: *18 white*   **SIZE:** *Doily 30 × 45cm (12 × 18")*   **DESIGNER:** *Ingrid Plum*

86

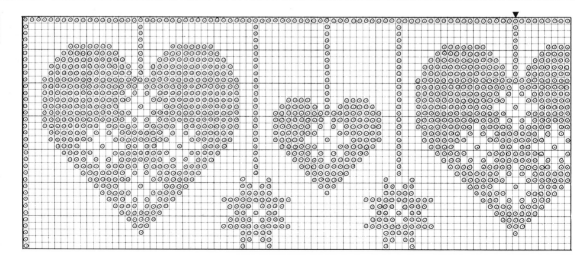

PAGE: *16*
FABRIC: *30 white*
SIZE: *Napkin 15 × 15cm*
(6 × 6")
DESIGNER: *Ida Winckler*

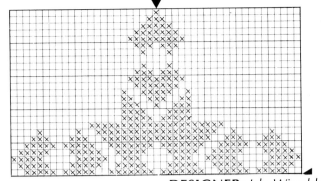 86

DESIGNER: *Ida Winckler*

PAGE: *16*

FABRIC: *30 white*   **SIZE:** *Runner 27 × 87cm (10½ × 34¼")*

86

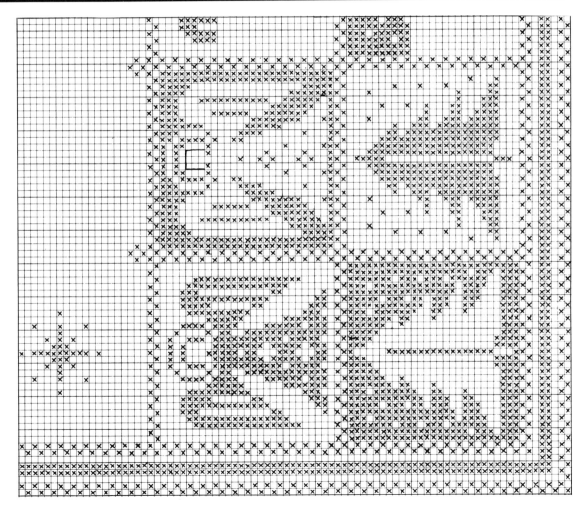

49

TECHNIQUE

Find the middle of the short side of the fabric. Measure 5cm (2") up from edge. Start the embroidery at the arrow on the pattern.
The edging is 78cm (30½") long.
The symbol / represents half cross stitches worked in one direction.

FINISHING

Trim fabric to 21 threads from embroidery. Turn under a double hem, 7 threads deep, 7 threads from the embroidery, and sew it in place with small hemming stitches.

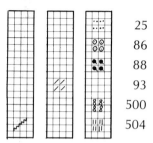

			25
			86
			88
			93
			500
			504

PAGE: *17*

FABRIC: *26 white*   **SIZE:** *Runner 22 × 100cm (8½ × 39½")*   **DESIGNER:** *Edith Hansen*

FINISHING

Trim fabric to 21 threads from embroidery. Turn under a double hem, 7 threads deep, 7 threads from the embroidery, and sew it in place with small hemming stitches.

97
504

PAGE: *19*
FABRIC: *26 white*
SIZE: *3.5 × 5.5cm*
      (1½ × 2¼")
DESIGNER: *Gerda Bengtsson*

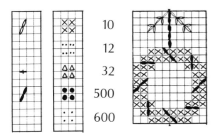

10
12
32
500
600

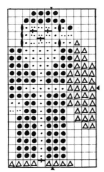

PAGE: *19*
FABRIC: *30 white*
SIZE: *19.5 × 23.5cm*
(7½ × 9¼")
DESIGNER: *Ida Winckler*

FINISHING

Mount on cardboard, either glueing edges to back or lacing them with herringbone stitch.

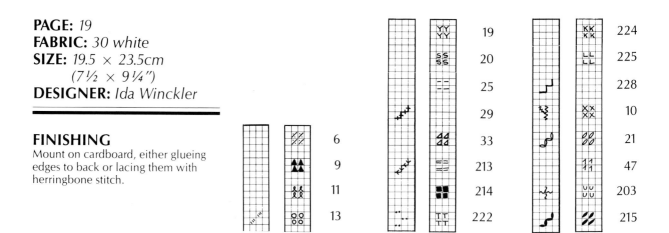

	6
▲▲	9
♣♣	11
○○	13

	19
⌇⌇	20
--	25
	29
⊿⊿	33
==	213
■■	214
TT	222

Y Y	19

KK	224
LL	225
	228
XX	10
○○	21
11	47
UU	203
⟋⟋	215

PAGE: *18*
FABRIC: *26 white*
SIZE: *19.5 × 22cm*
      (7½ × 8¾")
DESIGNER: *Ida Winckler*

FINISHING
Mount on cardboard.

✗✗	10		LL	88
ℓℓ	11		○○	96
✗✗	19			203
II	21		‡	215
∴	25			222
11	48		↓	100

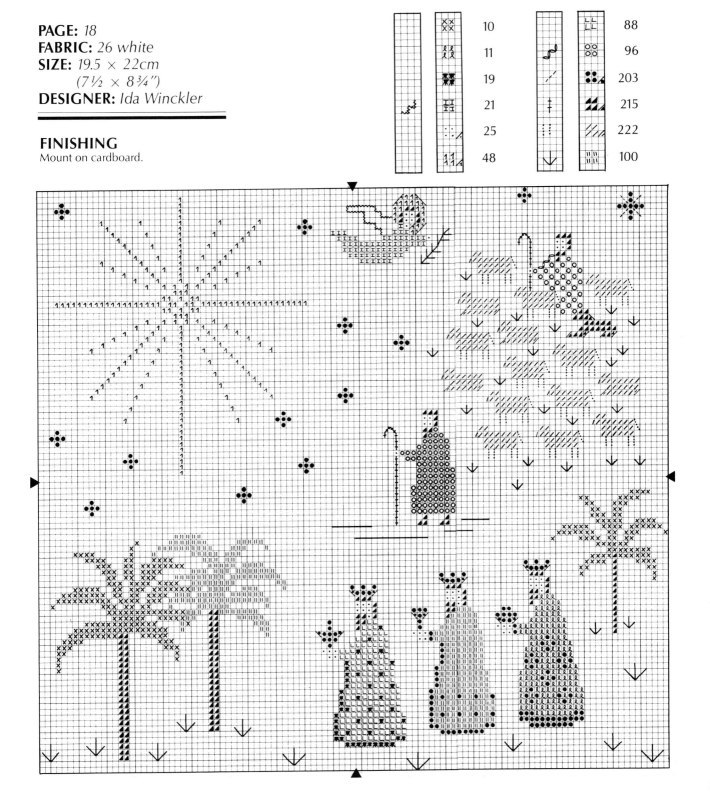

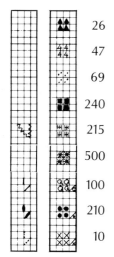

▲▲		26
44 / 44		47
∴		69
■■		240
⌗⌗		215
✳✳		500
໑໑		100
●●		210
✕✕		10

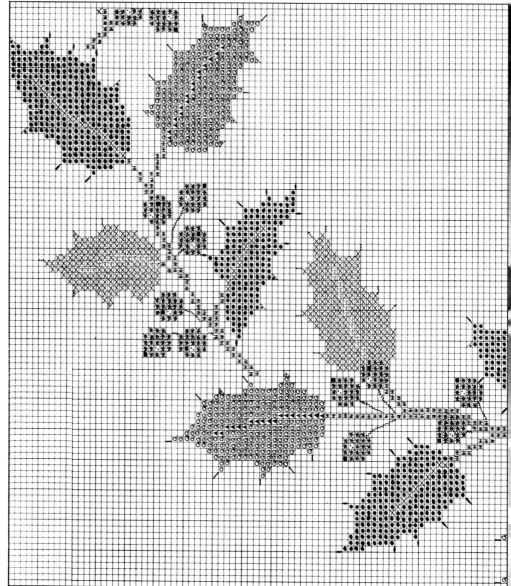

FINISHING

Make circular template, using compass, measuring 2cm (¾") wider than finished size. Trim fabric to fit. Cut a 2.5cm (1") bias strip to fit edge. Machine stitch it to the circle, right sides together. Turn the strip to wrong side, press the seam, and hem the strip in place.

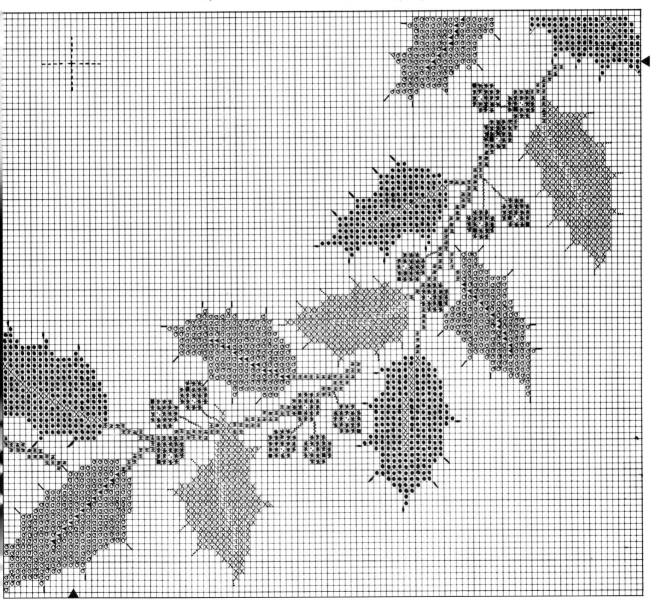

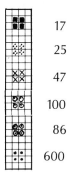

	17
	25
	47
	100
	86
	600

TECHNIQUE

Measure 3cm (1¼") in and to the right from left corner. Start the embroidery at the arrow on the pattern.

FINISHING

Trim fabric to 21 threads from embroidery. Turn under a double hem, 7 threads deep, 7 threads from the embroidery, and sew it in place with small stitches.

FABRIC: *26 white* **SIZE:** *Napkin 15 × 15cm (6 × 6")* **DESIGNER:** *Gerda Bengtsson*

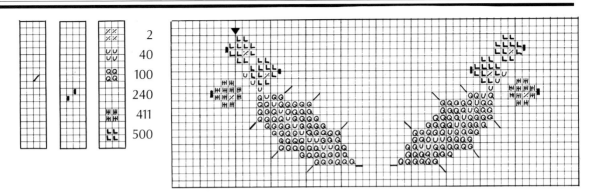

⊠⊠ / ⊠⊠	2
U U / U U	40
Q Q / Q Q	100
	240
H H / H H	411
L L / L L	500

PAGE: *19*

FABRIC: *26 white* **SIZE:** *Runner 13 × 80cm (5 × 31½")* **DESIGNER:** *Gerda Bengtsson*

TECHNIQUE

Find the middle of the short side of the fabric. Measure 5cm (2") up from edge. Start the embroidery at the arrow on the pattern.
The edging is about 77cm (30½") long.

FINISHING

Trim fabric to 18 threads from embroidery. Turn under a double hem, 7 threads deep, 4 threads from the embroidery, and sew it in place with small stitches.

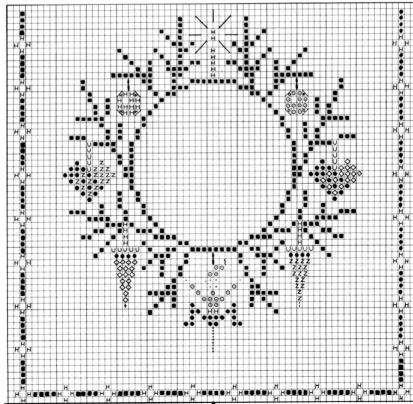

· · / · ·	12
● ● / ● ●	17
Z Z / Z Z	37
U U / U U	40
H H / H H	48
◇◇ / ◇◇	53
◎◎ / ◎◎	86
■ ■ / ■ ■	211

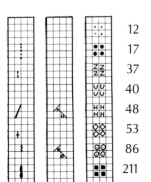

TECHNIQUE

Work with 2 strands of Danish Flower Thread or 4 strands of floss.

This motif and single repeat of cross and heart design (right) can be used for napkins.

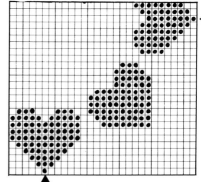

500

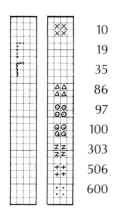

	10
	19
	35
	86
	97
	100
	303
	506
	600

PAGE: *20*
FABRIC: *26 white*
DESIGNER: *Ida Winckler*

TECHNIQUE

Work with 2 strands of Danish Flower Thread or 4 strands of floss.

FINISHING

Hem the runner with hemstitching worked over 3 threads, 8 threads deep.

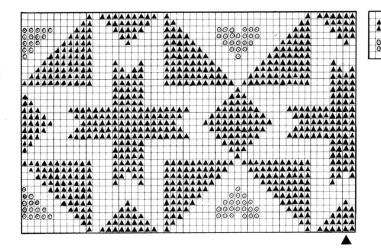

▲▲	17
○○	86

PAGE: *20*
DESIGNER: *Lisbeth K. Sørensen*

FABRIC: *18 white*
SIZE: *Placemat 30 × 42cm (12 × 16½")*

TECHNIQUE

Work with 2 strands of Danish Flower Thread or 4 strands of floss.

FINISHING

Trim fabric to 26 threads from embroidery. Turn under a double hem, 8 threads deep, 10 threads from the embroidery and sew in place.

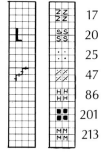

ZZ	17
SS	20
··	25
⁄⁄	47
HH	86
∷	201
MM	213

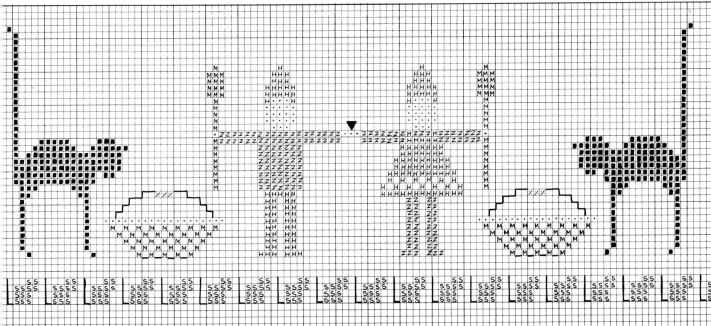

FABRIC: *26 white*   **SIZE:** *Diameter 5.5cm (2¼")*   **DESIGNER:** *Edith Hansen*

FINISHING

Work each motif twice as mirror images. Cut out 2 cardboard hearts from the shape given, and cut out the circle. Cut the embroidery to form a circle, diameter 6cm (2½"). Glue the embroideries under the cardboard hearts. Fasten a double thread at the top of one heart to hang up.
Glue the two hearts together with the embroideries back to back, first placing a piece of white paper between the embroideries to prevent any of the wrong side showing through.

17
21
229

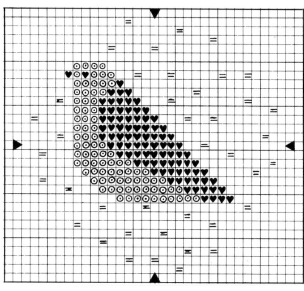

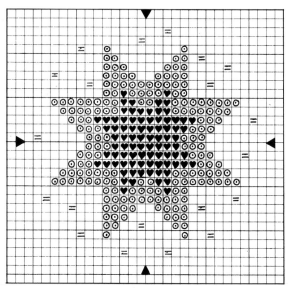

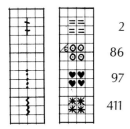

	==	2
	600	86
	♥♥	97
	✳✳	411

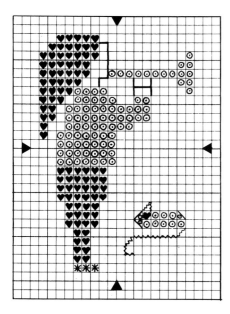

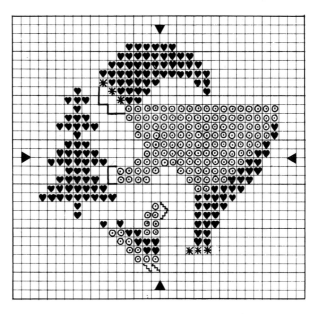

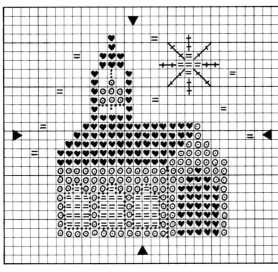

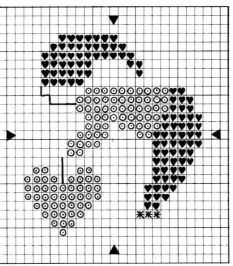

TECHNIQUE

Make a full size-shape in tracing paper, following the outline given on page 64. Find centre of fabric, place centre of shape over centre of fabric lengthwise. Tack (baste) the outline and centre line on the fabric, tear away the tracing paper gently. Start the embroidery at the arrow on the pattern. This point corresponds to the centre line on the fabric.

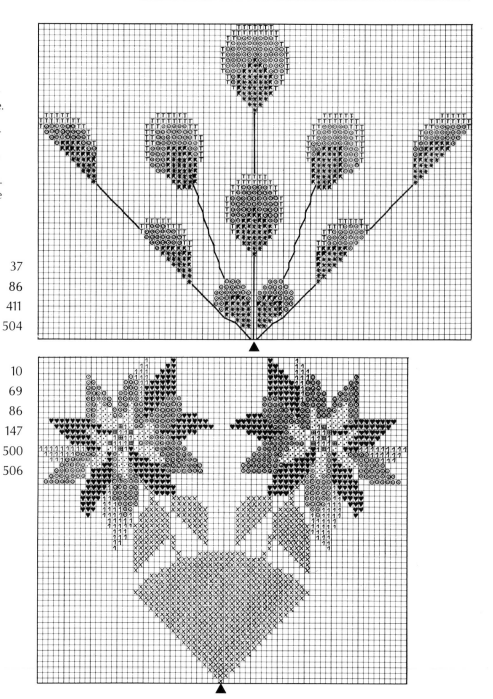

KK	37
OO	86
**	411
TT	504

XX	10
∴	69
OO	86
⊞⊞	147
♥♥	500
11	506